FREEMASONRY AND THE
CHRISTIAN FAITH

by
Fr Ashley Beck

*All booklets are published thanks to the
generous support of the members of the
Catholic Truth Society*

CATHOLIC TRUTH SOCIETY
PUBLISHERS TO THE HOLY SEE

CONTENTS

Acknowledgments

Among those who have read drafts I would like to thank in particular Monsignor Richard Moth, Father David Rhys, Michael Phelan, Michael Walsh, The Revd Canon Professor David Brown, the Revd Nick Wynne-Jones, Deacon Christopher Road, Paul Turner, and my parish priest Canon Jack Madden. I am also grateful to Martin Short for his helpful advice and encouragement and to my wife Caroline. Amongst my sources are the three most important books about the subject written in this country. The first is *Darkness Visible*, written in the 1950s by an Anglican cleric who later became a Catholic, Walton Hannah[1]; the sensational exposé written thirty years later, *The Brotherhood*, by Stephen Knight[2]; and its sequel by Martin Short, *Inside the Brotherhood*.[3] I would recommend these books for further reading and they are all still in print.

INTRODUCTION

Some years ago I was approached by a man who had been invited to become a Freemason. He wanted to know whether as a Catholic he was permitted to do so. I had not been a priest for very long and was not sure of the answer, although I found it out quickly; this booklet is an attempt to give a clear answer to the question and to explain some of the reasons for that answer.

The answer was, and is, a very firm 'no': Catholics are not permitted to be Freemasons. This booklet looks at what Freemasonry is and at Catholic teaching about it. We will also look at the place of Freemasonry within contemporary British society and how this relates to Catholic teaching about society. Although the primary focus is the position of Roman Catholics, we will also look briefly at the present relationship between Freemasonry and other churches.

The Catholic Church teaches that adherence to Freemasonry is incompatible with being a faithful Christian. For many people, including some members of other churches, this claim is painful and offensive, and it is very hard for an examination of this kind not to be seen simply as an attack; but I do hope that those who feel this will find this examination at least a balanced look at the evidence. Many Christian attacks on Freemasonry are irrational, unbalanced and superstitious; sometimes it is easier to attack some aspects of Freemasonry rather than others. Moreover we need to be aware that at times attacks on Freemasonry by Catholics, and others, have been linked to anti-Semitism.

Many Catholics, including the present writer, have good friends and family members who are Masons and it is not the purpose of this booklet to impugn the individual moral character of the majority of Masons. Rather, it is an examination of the *system* of Freemasonry: what it claims to believe, and how it operates.

This booklet has been written partly because about thirty years ago there was a brief period when Catholics in this country and the United States were told that they could be Masons, although this directive was then reversed; and since then it has not been easy to get hold of the authoritative teaching. Moreover the reasons behind the Church's teaching are not only important in themselves - they help us understand our faith more deeply. Although I will refer a little to Freemasonry in the rest of the world, my main focus will be on how it operates in Britain.

WHAT IS FREEMASONRY?

As Catholics we may well only have a hazy picture of
what Freemasonry actually is. It claims to be 'a peculiar
system of morality, veiled in allegory, and illustrated by
symbols.'[4] As a 'system' it is a society, the largest closed
or 'secret' society in the world - twenty years ago its size
was estimated to be about five million worldwide.
Secrecy is one of the things most people know about
Freemasonry even if they know nothing else, but what do
we mean when we say Freemasonry is 'secret'? There
are two ways in which the description applies: first, its
characteristic rituals are not only closed to those who are
not initiated Masons, but members have to swear not to
reveal details about them; second, although the names of
provincial and national officials are in the public domain,
the names of ordinary members themselves are kept
secret. This second feature is in itself unremarkable and
many clubs and societies do not publish membership
lists, but it is important with regard to Freemasonry
because of the secrecy of the rituals and the way in
which the organisation operates, or is perceived to
operate, in society.

Origins of English Freemasonry

What we understand as English Freemasonry dates from the year 1717, when the 'Grand Lodge' was founded. This was really the organised beginning of what is known as 'speculative' masonry, based on, and in some ways arising out of originally medieval (and Catholic) guilds of real stone Masons. These men had been grouped in tightly-knit societies to preserve their own identity and working practices: as Masons often had to move from area to area seeking building work, they needed to be recognised as 'professionals' by other Masons, so a system of recognisable passwords, signs and handgrips developed; similarly, like modern Trades unions, they were grouped in chapters or lodges. As with many craft guilds, the Masons would trace their lineage to figures in history, and (as one would expect in a Christian culture) this naturally related to accounts in the Old Testament of the building of the Temple in Jerusalem at the behest of Solomon, the son of King David. After the Reformation in England there was a sharp decline in new church building, so the networks of real (or 'operative', as they are known to Freemasons) Masons declined, and they bolstered their numbers by letting in others who had no idea of how to wield a trowel or a chisel; in time these outnumbered the original Masons, and by the beginning of the 18th century the lodges in London which formed 'Grand Lodge' were entirely made up of the nobility and gentry. For these men the symbols of masonry - compasses, square, stone, column, and so on - were used as guides for living a good moral life. Only men are allowed to become Masons, although there are linked societies for their children, and wives are often entertained at special social events known as 'ladies' nights'; there are Masonic-like organisations for women, or for men and women, but these are not considered part of mainstream Freemasonry, and a Mason who goes to their meetings can be subject to disciplinary action.

Lodges, officers and initiations

A 'lodge' is simply a group of Masons. Sometimes it is simply based in a geographical area; quite often it might be associated with a particular profession or workplace, or be linked to another grouping such as old boys of a school. Many Masons are members of a number of different lodges. A lodge may vary enormously in number from 20 to 400. The focal point of the lodge's official life is a variety of rituals, primarily concerned with 'opening' a lodge and initiating new members, and it is on this basis that it has to have officers to run it who are elected annually - the 'Worshipful Master', together with two 'Wardens', and two Deacons to assist the Master. There is a figure known as the 'Tyler' who keeps guard outside the lodge with a drawn sword to stop outsiders from getting in. There is also a 'Standard bearer' and a 'Chaplain' (not necessarily a clergyman), and an organist, together with more conventional officers such as a Secretary, a Treasurer, a Master of Ceremonies and an Almoner, who deals with the charitable giving. 'Past Masters' are also important. Lodges in a particular area, usually a county or part of a county, are grouped into provinces, and 'Grand Lodge' is the principal national grouping. At each of these levels there are the same officers as in an ordinary lodge, with 'provincial' or 'grand' rank, and these officers are in different ways the public face of the organisation. Grand Lodge is based in an imposing building (without ground floor windows) in Great Queen Street in Covent Garden, near which are a number of Masonic shops. The organisation as a whole is often simply referred to as 'The Craft'.

The term 'lodge' is used to describe the room within which the rituals take place - the main room in Masonic halls or 'temples' which the organisation owns for its gatherings. The lodge has a distinctive chequered floor and ornaments. Most Freemasonry is centred, or (as it is known) 'worked' in three *degrees*: Entered Apprentice, Fellow Craft and Master Mason. A Mason has to be initiated to each degree after a short space of time - each one has a distinctive apron, hand grip, password, symbols, and a tracing board which is displayed in the lodge. The rituals are all based on a mythical reconstruction of the life and death of the Mason Hiram Abiff in relation to the building of the Temple; there are also many demonstrations of secret signs and steps around the floor;

the lodge is also decorated with pillars and the symbolic Masons' tools. There are many 'lectures' given by the master to the candidate, and those taking part are expected to learn their parts off by heart. It has been claimed that one can sometimes see Masons trying to learn their lines from printed rituals while sitting in railway carriages. Masons claim that the ritual is very moving (and it is often accompanied by organ music), although of course it is not possible for others to evaluate this claim.

Traditionally Masons are 'chosen' - a discreet approach is made to someone thought to be suitable, and he has to be approved by the lodge membership, although there are grounds for thinking that in recent years it has become easier to join. Lodges are famous too for their social life which takes place after the formal gathering - what is known as the 'festive board'. Masons usually wear suits and black neck ties under their regalia; as they often carry what they need while going to meetings in black attache cases they are fairly distinctive in the areas near Masonic halls and temples, particularly in the late afternoon.

Oath of Secrecy

A keynote is secrecy. At each degree a candidate has to swear - formerly (until 1986) under pain of dire physical penalties - not to reveal to outsiders the details of the rituals, passwords or other things which are revealed during the rituals. They have long been 'leaked' and published by others (particularly since Hannah's book was published in the 1950) but Masons are still expected to change the subject if you try and talk to them about what goes on. Some of the secret things are used as subtle ways of making oneself known to other Masons, such as the handgrip, not to mention phrases such as 'working tools' referring to cutlery at meals and expressions such as 'on the square' or 'on the level' which have also become common in ordinary English usage. Examples are sometimes cited of phrases (such as 'Come to my assistance, ye children of the widow' or 'I call upon the Great Architect to save me in this hour')[5] or secret signs being used in public settings such as a courtroom chambers to elicit support from other Masons (such as the magistrate or the judge) for the speaker.

Beliefs

In English-speaking and 'Germanic' Freemasonry (that is, in the British Isles, the Commonwealth, the United States and northern Europe) a candidate is expected to believe in a 'supreme being': God is referred to in Masonic literature, rituals and prayers as 'The Great Architect Of The Universe' (traditionally abbreviated in Masonic rituals to 'T.G.A.O.T.U'), or (in the 'Second degree') the 'Grand Geometrician', or 'The Most High'. Freemasonry in France, Italy, the rest of southern Europe and Latin America, abandoned this requirement in 1877 and Grand Lodge in England broke off relations at that point; non-English

Freemasonry has often been characterised by militant atheism and opposition to Christianity and to the Catholic Church in particular. It is known as the 'Grand Orient'. Freemasonry was born in the 18th century, an era in which religious belief declined in most of Europe, and in which there was a reaction to the conflicts and intolerance of the previous centuries. So English-speaking Freemasonry has formed a basic belief in God, as 'lowest common denominator', a belief which can in theory encompass all varieties of Christian, Jews, Muslims and others. Beyond this, discussion of religion (and politics) is forbidden in lodges. Oaths are sworn on what is called the 'Volume of Sacred Law' (V.S.L.) which is usually (in England) the Bible, but which can be the Jewish Bible or the Koran. Masonic prayers, even when based on Christian prayers, remove any reference to Jesus. Masons have their own system of dating years according to the *anno lucis* ('year of light') reckoned from the date for the creation of the world worked out by the Irish Archbishop Ussher - 4004 BC, rounded up to 4000. So AD 2005 is 'AL' 6005. A Mason's son is known as a 'lewis' and his brother is termed a 'martin'; those who are not Masons are called 'cowans' or 'the profane.'

Degrees within Freemasonry

Most Masons are solely involved in Freemasonry in the three 'degrees' referred to above. But there are other higher degrees, to which only 'Master Masons' can be admitted;

in general these encompass more serious Masons and the numbers are fewer. The most important is known as the 'Holy Royal Arch', which bases its rituals on the building of the Second Temple after the return of the people of Israel from the exile in Babylon. Its members are termed 'companions' and they are grouped in 'chapters' rather than lodges; a Royal Arch chapter's officials are named after the figures in the Old Testament account: Zerubbabel, Haggai, Joshua, Ezra and Nehemiah (in Ireland it is based on the completely different account of Josiah recovering the book of the Law). The Royal Arch considers itself to be a superior kind of Freemasonry, containing its 'essence'. Another degree which is to be found in England is the 'Mark Masons', whose rituals are based on accounts describing the Overseers of the ordinary Masons in the building of the Temple, and 'Royal Ark Mariner' degree, which is based on the story of Noah's Ark.

The best-known of the other higher degrees is the 18th, the 'Rose Croix of Heredom', and, at least in the past, this has been popular with Masons who were practising Christians and was reserved to them. The ceremonial for this degree is very elaborate and unusual, involving at one stage what seems to be a parody of the Mass and the burning of chemicals within a chalice to produce a rose-red flame; the rituals for this degree are based not on Old Testament events but on the crucifixion of Our Lord. Masonic higher degrees also include the Orders of Knight Templar and the Knights of Malta: for these one has to profess belief in the Holy Trinity. These Masonic degrees are modern inventions by Freemasonry and it should be stressed that they have nothing whatever to do with ancient Catholic orders of knighthood such as the Sovereign and Military Order of St John of Jerusalem or the Sovereign Military Order of Malta. Nor is Freemasonry linked to the St John's Ambulance Brigade, although it does make charitable donations to it.

As I indicated above, a feature of most of these ceremonies are the lectures given by senior officials to the person being initiated to each particular degree. These 'charges', as they are sometimes called, explain in detail Masonic symbolism and give a very clear picture of the Masonic system of beliefs.

These are the most important degrees or orders which in their rituals provide the focal point for Freemasonry. Of course for many Masons the social life and companionship which follows these ceremonies is what really matters; as some commentators have pointed out, for men in busy professional lives the evening at the Lodge, away from family responsibilities, can offer an attractive social setting, perhaps with opportunities to reminisce about times at school (if it is an old boys' Lodge) and to get to know well similar people in the local community in an environment which is private, where people can speak freely about uncontroversial subjects.

Charitable giving

As I said in my introduction another feature of Lodge life
is charitable giving. Some of this, quite naturally, is
focussed on Masons who are in need or their families:
striking examples of what has been done are the Royal
Masonic Hospital in west London and schools for the
children of Masons (although the one for boys closed in
1977). Freemasons do give a great deal to non-Masonic
causes such as those which support refugees in different
parts of the world. As we shall discuss below, however,
there are some disconcerting aspects to charitable giving
within Freemasonry.

Another thing to be aware of is a Mason's obligation to
help other Masons. This is what is said in one of the
'charges' read to a new Master Mason by the Master:

> 'Hand to hand I greet you as a brother; foot to foot I
> will support you in all your undertakings; knee to
> knee, the posture of my daily supplications shall
> remind me of all your wants; breast to breast, your
> lawful secrets when entrusted to me as such I will
> keep as my own; and hand over back, I will support
> your character in your absence as in your presence'[6]

Since the 1980s the leadership of the organisation has
been conscious of the need to portray itself in a better
light, following the exposures of scandals by the books

written by Knight and Short. As we shall examine below, at about this time the dire penalties in the Masonic oaths were removed; in 1988 a video was published to portray the Craft favourably to the general population, and a permanent public exhibition was opened by the Grand Master, the Duke of Kent, in Freemasons' Hall, and public tours of it are now organised.[7] In 2002 it was reported that Grand Lodge had employed a public relations consultant who was not a Mason in order to improve its image.[8] Also in that year there was held a *Week of Masonic Openness* from 26th June until 2nd July.[9] A sustained campaign was undertaken to present the organisation positively in the public eye; the same effort is made by Masonic websites to provide an attractive introduction to the Craft.

Freemasonry is a serious business which is valued by its members. Partly because of the secrecy it has always been easy to be flippant about the rituals, but we should acknowledge that it demands a great deal of commitment from its adherents. I have tried in this section to give a simple and clear picture of what Freemasonry is about.

Catholic Teaching about Freemasonry

Roman Catholics are forbidden from becoming Freemasons. This is the text of the *Declaration on Masonic Associations*, issued by the Sacred Congregation for the Doctrine of the Faith on 26th November 1983:

'The question has been asked whether the view of the Church in regard to Freemasonry has been changed by reason of the fact that there is no express mention of the same in the new Code of Canon Law, as there was in the previous code.

This Sacred Congregation is able to reply that the circumstance indicated is due to an editorial policy which has been followed in regard to other associations as well, which have similarly not been mentioned inasmuch as they are included in broader categories.

Therefore, the negative position of the Church in regard to Masonic associations remains unchanged, since their basic principles have always been considered irreconcilable with the teachings of the Church, and consequently, membership of them remains forbidden. The faithful who belong to

Masonic associations are in a state of grave sin and may not receive Holy Communion.

It is not within the competence of local church authorities to pass judgement on the nature of Masonic associations in such a way as to derogate from what has been established above; this is in line with the declaration of this Sacred Congregation issued on 17th February 1981.[10]

The Supreme Pontiff, John Paul II, in the course of the audience given to the undersigned Cardinal Prefect, approved the present Declaration, which was decided upon in the ordinary meeting of this Sacred Congregation, and has ordered its publication.'[11]

The document was signed by the then Prefect of the Sacred Congregation for the Doctrine of the Faith, Cardinal Joseph Ratzinger, now Pope Benedict XVI.

It is clear and unambiguous: you cannot be a Freemason and a Catholic in good standing with the Church. This declaration followed a long line of papal condemnations of the Craft, starting with Clement XII's Apostolic letter *In Eminenti Apostolatus Specula* (1738),[12] not long after the foundation of the Grand Lodge, and subsequent statements by various Popes.[13] In the 1917 *Code of Canon Law*, Freemasonry was specifically mentioned as an organisation which plotted against the

Church; automatic excommunication is incurred by 'those who enrol in the Masonic sect or in other organisations of the same sort which plot against the Church or the legitimate civil authorities.'[14] The 1983 statement was necessary for two reasons.

Code of Canon Law

The first reason is to do with the new *Code of Canon Law* issued in 1983. In its section on *Offences against Church Authorities* it makes it clear that a Catholic who joins 'an association which plots against the Church is to be punished with a just penalty. One who promotes or takes office in such an association is to be punished with an interdict.'[15] This replaced the canon in the 1917 code quoted above. During the drafting process, in 1981 the Sacred Congregation for the Doctrine of the Faith made it clear that no significance should be read into the fact that it was no longer mentioned by name: it was still covered. The above declaration was issued in 1983 on the day before the new code was promulgated.

Clarification required

The second is that in the 1970s, in a number of places, Catholics were told that they were not subject to the canonical penalty and could become Masons under certain circumstances. In a letter to certain bishops in 1974 from the then Prefect of the Sacred Congregation for the Doctrine

of the Faith, Cardinal Franjo Seper, it was pointed out that
Masons might not be automatically excommunicated by the
provision in the 1917 code.[16] A subsequent statement by the
Bishops' Conference of England and Wales, and parallel
decisions made by individual bishops in the United States,
allowed Catholics to be Masons if local Freemasons in a
particular area were not known to be hostile to the Church.[17]
In England there had been some contacts from the late
1960s between the then Archbishop of Westminster,
Cardinal John Heenan, and influential Masons with the aim
of reviewing the ban. The change of attitude and the wish to
be lenient was based on the distinction which we have
already noted between 'Grand Lodge' masonry (English,
Irish, American and northern European) and that known as
the 'Grand Orient' (French, Italian and Latin American)
over belief in God. The view was taken that because the
'Grand Lodge' was not atheist, it was not a threat or an
opponent of the Catholic Church. It is likely that in this
period (from 1974 until at least 1981) a number of
Catholics, at least in Britain and the United States, became
Masons in good faith.[18]

The 1981 statement made it clear that the canonical
position had not in fact changed; it was soon clarified again
that the problem is not to do with whether Masons believe in
God, or whether the organisation has conspired against the
Church in political life, but the fundamental theological
outlook which it promotes. Indeed, papal condemnations

from the earliest stages focussed on the theology of English 'Grand Lodge' Freemasonry, since at that stage there was no distinction between the 'Grand Lodge' and the 'Grand Orient'. This theological outlook, presented in Masonic rituals, is inconsistent with Christianity. This had been clear in earlier papal condemnations; it was also elucidated in an article in the Vatican newspaper *L'Osservatore Romano*.[19] After the 1983 declaration was published, details were forwarded to clergy in England and Wales by the bishops. In the United States a detailed statement was issued by the Catholic Bishops' Conference which explained many of the reasons.[20] What the 1983 declaration made clear in particular was that local circumstances such as the attitudes of local lodges made no difference to the position and that local bishops could not dispense people from the prohibition, and it effectively nullified Cardinal Seper's 1974 letter.

We will look now at the three principal reasons for this teaching:

(i) Freemasonry is a naturalistic religion

Although Freemasonry claims to be 'neither a religion nor a substitute for religion'[21], this claim is disingenuous. More honest Masonic writers, such as Albert Pike (in works such as *Morals and Dogma of the Antient and Accepted Scottish Rite of Freemasonry*, 1882) and Albert G. Mackey (in his *Encyclopedia of Freemasonry*, London: 1908 and other works), have acknowledged that it has all the attributes of a religion: temples, altars, prayers, a moral code, worship, vestments, feast days, the promise of reward or punishment in an after-life ('the Grand Lodge above'), and a hierarchy; if it isn't a religion, what would it need to be one? And in the religious ideology promoted in the lectures and rituals, it is clear that the candidate is seen as one progressing from darkness and ignorance into light and knowledge through his own efforts and the use of symbols of morality. Here are three examples:

First, these words are said by the Worshipful Master at the ceremony of raising a Mason to the 'second degree', that of Fellow Craft:

'... By square conduct, level steps and upright intentions we hope to ascend to those immortal mansions whence all goodness emanates.'[22]

Second, this prayer is said at the beginning of the ceremony of raising a Mason to the 'third degree', that of Master Mason:

'... Endue [thy servant] with such fortitude that in the hour of trial he fail not, but that, passing safely under thy protection through the valley of the shadow of death, he may finally rise from the tomb of transgression, to shine as the stars for ever and ever.'[23]

Finally, a little later on in the same ceremony, the Worshipful Master says this to the candidate:

> *(He is referring back to what had been imparted in the second degree)* 'The secrets of nature and the principles of intellectual truth were then unveiled to your view. To your mind, thus modelled by virtue and science, Nature, however, presents one great and useful lesson more. She prepares you, by contemplation, for the closing hour of existence; and when by means of that contemplation she has conducted you through the intricate workings of this mortal life, she finally instructs you how to die.'[24]

These three examples show two related aspects of Masonic theology and anthropology. First, the Mason advances in knowledge, hidden from most people, as a result of his own efforts and moral qualities; and second, that the source of this knowledge is not a personal relationship with God but simply 'nature'. This was what in the nineteenth century Pope Leo XIII in his encyclical on Freemasonry, *Humanum Genus*, had to say about 'naturalism', or 'nature religion':

> 'Now the fundamental doctrine of the naturalists, which they sufficiently make known by their very name, is that human nature and human reason ought in all things be mistress and guide... For they deny

that anything has been taught by God; they allow no dogma or religion or truth which cannot be understood by human intelligence nor any teacher who ought to be believed by reason of his authority.'[25]

This is the problem with the symbols which are endlessly put before the Mason as representing moral qualities - the compass, set square and so on. Geometry and architectural proportion are from the world of nature - these are seen as the best moral guides rather than any revelation from God. Some of the symbols are put on the 'Volume of Sacred Law', and the many oaths are sworn on it, but it remains largely a symbol rather than a source of teaching, since if it were to be used as a source of teaching, divisions within the lodge between Christians and others would soon arise.

Emphasis on effort

The whole system of progress from one degree to another is heavy with emphasis on the Mason passing through stages as a result of his own efforts: for those unable to see Masonic rituals, one of the most illuminating portrayals of this are the trials of Tamino and Papageno in Mozart's opera *The Magic Flute*. God's grace doesn't come into it; this is not surprising, because in the 18th century, when these rituals were developed, a view of God was formed which we call 'deist'; this sees God essentially simply as a creator, no longer closely involved with the world after it has been made - as an Architect. This view was an attempt to move away from theological disputes which had led to religious wars, and is associated with the French philosopher Voltaire. God is so distant from us that we cannot really know him; that is why one of the most popular hymns among Masons is 'Immortal, Invisible, God only wise; in light inaccessible, hid from our eyes...'[26] The remoteness of the 'Great Architect' means that the Mason only has his symbols rather than any knowledge of absolute truth.

In 1980, after six years of research and dialogue with Freemasonry, the Catholic bishops of West Germany reached this conclusion:

> 'The religious conception of the Mason is relativistic. All religions are competitive attempts to explain the truth about God which, in the last analysis, is unattainable. Therefore, only the language of Masonic symbols, which is ambiguous and left to the subjective interpretation of the individual Mason, is adapted to this truth about God.'[27]

There is an old saying, 'The Englishman believes that there is no God, but that it is wise to pray to him from time to time.' Much of what goes in Freemasonry seems to fit in with this; God is there, but *out there*, rather a long way off. This whole emphasis on the Mason's personal progress to

illumination by his own efforts in many ways makes
Freemasonry the natural religion of the 'self-made'
successful professional, the *entrepreneur*: he has done well,
he works hard, and he believes that this is due to his own
efforts. The Lodge is largely full of men who are like him; the
spiritual side of their lives, enriched with symbols of hard and
careful physical work, reflects the same system of rewards
for effort, rewards for an elite. This makes Freemasonry
rather like Pelagianism, the 5th century heresy which taught
that humanity could achieve perfection through good works;
it is also a form of the earlier 2nd century heresy of
Gnosticism, in which people were taught that they could
attain salvation through acquiring secret knowledge, *gnosis*.

Evidence of Pelagianism

Pelagianism is illustrated further if we look at one of the
things which many will agree is a commendable
characteristic of the Craft, the charitable giving of
Freemasons at national and local levels. The good aspects
of this should be recognised, especially in terms of gifts
made to non-Masonic causes[28], although one reason more
is known about this is that the Craft has made sure in
recent years that these gifts have been made very
publicly. But within Freemasonry there is a system of
recognising how much individual brothers give, the award
of the 'Charity Jewel'- medals and bars on medals are
awarded according to specific sums of money given[29];

these Jewels are highly sought after. This contrasts blatantly with the injunctions of Jesus in the Sermon on the Mount, read in church every Ash Wednesday:

> 'Be careful not to parade your deeds before men to attract their notice; by doing this you will lose all reward from your Father in heaven. So when you give alms, do not have it trumpeted before you; this is what the hypocrites do in the synagogues and in the streets to win men's admiration. I tell you most solemnly, they have had their reward. But when you give alms, your left hand must not know what your right hand is doing; your almsgiving must be secret, and your Father who sees all that is done in secret will reward you.'[30]

To make matters worse, the ideology of a Mason's individual approach to charitable giving is distinctly unsacrificial, even though a willingness and ability to give is expected of every Mason; for in the third-degree obligation, the aspiring Master Mason pledges himself to help his brother 'so far as may fairly be done without detriment to myself or my connections.'[31] Do Christian Masons really think this calculating approach is consistent with the teachings of Jesus in the Sermon on the Mount, or the lives of the saints of the Christian Church?

The Masonic world-view is incompatible with Christianity. The Mason has no real need of grace, because he has done it all himself; moreover the figure of the suffering Christ on the Cross, vulnerable and weak, is an alien symbol which says nothing to him which he wants to hear - the Mason's faith is essentially *anthropocentric*, centred on man. Everybody else, even the 'Great Architect', is in the background, a long way off. That is why the 'social side' of Freemasonry, which so many Masons claim is what really matters, cannot be detached from the rituals or the theology of the organisation - the nature of the community, and what is meant in terms of those who are excluded from it, is central to what it is all about. By contrast Christianity teaches that God offers salvation to all people, not simply to those men who have been chosen to be in a lodge - that is why Christian worship is open to all, not conducted in secret. The whole emphasis we have examined goes a long way towards explaining the secrecy: if the path to a good moral life is only open to a few, then you have to keep everyone else out. The contempt for others which this shows, reflected in all the ways in which Masons are exhorted to avoid discussing their beliefs and rituals with 'cowans', is not an added extra: it is at the heart of the whole ideology.

(ii) Freemasonry is a religion which excludes Christ

'Almighty God, unto whom all hearts be open, all desires known, and from whom no secrets are hid; cleanse the thoughts of our hearts by the inspiration of thy Holy Spirit, that we may perfectly love thee, and worthily magnify thy holy name. SO MOTE IT BE.'[32]

This is a prayer often used at Masonic meetings, which closely resembles the 'Collect for Purity', one of the best known of all prayers in the English language, from the Book of Common Prayer of the Church of England. But there are two differences: 'So mote it be' replaces 'Amen', and the words 'Through Christ our Lord' have been removed. So it is in all Masonic worship - references to Christ, or to the Trinity, are removed from traditional prayers and texts such as the psalms.

This is what is said when a candidate first comes for initiation as a Freemason:

'Mr...a poor candidate in a state of darkness who has been well and worthily recommended, and regularly proposed and approved in open Lodge, now comes of his own free will and accord, properly prepared, humbly soliciting to be admitted to the mysteries and privileges of Freemasonry.'[33]

When he comes into the lodge this man in a state of darkness is wearing simply a shirt unbuttoned to exposed his left breast, his trousers with the left leg rolled up above the knee, having had all metal objects removed; in place of his right shoe he is wearing a slipper, a noose of silk is around his neck and he is blindfolded.

Christians assert that Jesus is 'the Way, the Truth and the Life' - the Incarnation puts Jesus at the centre of human existence, and we can never allow him to be sidelined. How can *a baptised Christian*, who has been given new birth through his baptism, who has been *enlightened by Christ*, allow himself to be portrayed as being in a state of darkness and go through this ritual?

Exclusion of Christian references

The medieval guilds of 'operative' Masons, that is, men who earned their living by cutting stone, were of course Catholic. Their craft was centred on the building of churches and cathedrals for the worship of God and the sacramental life of the Church. The history of 'speculative' Freemasonry in its early decades in the 18th century makes it clear that a definite decision was taken, as various rituals were standardised, to de-Christianise them to remove references to Christ: the aim was to 'oblige them to that Religion to which all men agree, leaving their particular opinions to themselves.'[34] This enabled lodges to admit Jews and (in theory) Muslims, indeed anyone who is able simply to profess a belief in God. The position of Christ is seen as a source of dissension and division in the Lodge, and that is why discussion of religion (and politics) is forbidden in lodges. Although there was a schism within Freemasonry which partly related to this de-Christianisation, by the time the

'United Grand Lodge' was formed in 1813 and the schism healed, this was universally accepted in the basic three Craft degrees.[35] The Craft seeks its models and symbols elsewhere. For example, in the third degree initiation rite, for the Master Mason, it is the story of the death of the Mason Hiram Abiff which is re-enacted by the candidate to symbolise his coming to new life; it is re-enacted very vividly, with the blindfolded candidate being lowered into and raised from a mock coffin on the floor (either depicted on a cloth, or sometimes a real box within a trap-door). For any Christian to do this is incomprehensible: in Christ, through our baptism, we enter into his victory over death, we do not need to have it symbolically re-enacted in some other way, and to do so detracts from what is for his disciples the central event in human history.

Rituals and degrees

The 'Holy Royal Arch' degree is seen by Masons, or at least by its own 'companions', as an elite form of Freemasonry, and has often presented as a degree particularly appropriate for Christians which in the past has included many clergy. The initiation ritual centres on the search for the name of God, represented by a series of brass letters in Hebrew and English on an altar, jumbled up and then rearranged. Until comparatively recently, in the Royal Arch ceremonies, the Hebrew name for God from the Old Testament is conflated with the Canaanite deity Baal and the Egyptian god Osiris to form the name 'JAH-BUL-ON'. As has often been pointed out in terms of the theology of the Bible, this is blasphemous: why, in the Second Book of Kings, did Elijah and Jehu go to the trouble of fighting so hard against the priests of Baal, if everyone was worshipping the same God? We see from this that not only does this moral system claim to sidestep the distinctions between religions, but that the distinctions do not matter at all. Following controversy in the 1980s in England Grand Chapter (the supreme body in Royal Arch masonry) removed the name 'JAH-BUL-ON' from the rituals in 1989[36]; but it is clear that this concept of the universal name is still central to what the Royal Arch is about. Again, Christ the light of the world is nowhere to be seen.

At least one of the so-called 'Christian degrees' is actually worse still: the rituals of the 'Rose Croix' 18th degree, referred to above, use the crucifixion of Our Lord in a way which turns Christianity into a man-centred mystery religion. As Hannah puts it, 'Our Lord's redemptive death is treated as a type and an allegory of the experiences which a Mason must undergo in his quest for light, not as a unique and objective act of redemption wrought for him by God.'[37] In Freemasonry not only is Christ entirely absent from the basic three degrees, when he does appear in the higher, elite degrees, his place in the salvation history of mankind is parodied. In the macabre rites of the Knights Templar degree (for which belief in the Holy Trinity is a requirement) all that the Masonic world-view can find in Christian history as a symbol is the violence and militarism of the crusades.[38] By contrast in some of the other higher or 'Scottish Rite' degrees, particularly important in the United States, the anti-Christian imagery is very explicit.[39]

Concept of Deity

The God of Freemasons, depicted as an architect or a geometrician, is a 'lowest common denominator', a deity reduced to the barest of attributes so as to be above human dissension and the disagreements which religion so often brings: he is also removed from human life and a figure whom men cannot know. If some of what has been described above seems inconsistent, that is no accident: each Mason can make what he likes of his God. Christian teaching about the Incarnation, in which the gulf between God and humanity is bridged for ever by the person of Jesus Christ, is a serious threat to the whole Masonic belief system. The Christian faith of the Christian Mason becomes incidental: it does not need to be there. Moreover we know that this has not happened by accident - it is a deliberate distortion and devaluation of the Christian faith, and it remains shocking that over the last two and a half centuries so many Christians, including many senior clergy of different churches, have colluded with this.

There are now circumstances in which Christians can offer prayers with members of other faiths: the late Pope John Paul II did so in Italy at special acts of witness for peace in the world. But these are special events, and are never allowed to detract from our faith in the uniqueness of Christ and our belief that he alone is the source of salvation. The contrast between what Christian Masons accept and mainstream Christian belief is even clearer if we reflect on the experience of martyrdom in the life of the Church - if faith in Christ is not essential, why should it cost you your life? A Mason, asked to sacrifice to the gods of ancient Rome, would be able to do so cheerfully, believing that such things do not really matter.

By contrast with the Masonic world view, this is how the Church frequently prays at Mass on Sundays:

> 'Father, all powerful and ever-living God, we do
> well always and everywhere to give you thanks
> through Jesus Christ our Lord.
> Through his cross and resurrection he freed us from
> sin and death
> and called us to the glory that has made us a chosen
> race, a royal priesthood,
> a holy nation, a people set apart.
> Everywhere we proclaim your mighty works
> for you have called us out of darkness into your
> own wonderful light...'[40]

It is through the cross and resurrection of Christ that humanity is led from darkness and offered the gift of light; and these 'mighty works' are proclaimed everywhere, not hidden behind locked doors in buildings without windows.

These few lines encapsulate the *profound difference* between Freemasonry and Christianity.

(iii) The oaths of Freemasonry

For many years opponents of Freemasonry drew attention to the dire physical penalties which the candidate for different degrees calls down on himself should he reveal any secrets - having his throat cut, his head cut off, and worse. The Craft's apologists are apt to explain that these, like everything else, are purely symbolic, and were common in oaths in the 18th century; Grand Lodge, concerned at the public's perception, removed the penalties in England in 1986. But if the authorities of Freemasonry thought that removing this violence from the oaths would remove the objections to them, they missed the point: the point of a dagger is still at the candidate's chest, and the violence is still there. The problem with the oaths, in traditional Christian moral theology, is that you cannot swear an oath on the Bible, in the name of God, in relation to things which you do not yet know. For Catholics, the *Code of Canon Law* makes this clear:

> 'An oath is the invocation of the divine Name as witness to the truth. It cannot be taken except in truth, judgement and justice… An oath extorted by deceit, force or grave fear is by virtue of the law itself invalid.'[41]

The candidate does not yet know the alleged 'secrets' - to extract an oath in such a way is a false pretence, a deception, and such an oath has no validity.[42] If he is not serious, the sin is even worse, because of the solemnity, the use of God's name and the Bible. And yet in the drama of the various initiation ceremonies, these grotesque and violent statements have been something of a highlight, and indeed there was controversy among Masons when they were removed twenty years ago.

The true force of masonic ritual

These are the three *fundamental* theological reasons for the teaching of the Catholic Church; they are to do with what Freemasonry makes clear in its rituals and charges. It is quite incorrect to allege that the reasons are to do with political antagonism between the Church and Freemasonry. Masons often claim that their critics read too much into these ceremonies, and that they are not really that important; most members, it is argued, simply go along with all this because of the rest of what being a Freemason is about: the *camaraderie*, generous hospitality, giving to charity, meeting similar people. As a defence this is pretty threadbare. These rituals are conducted in an air of real solemnity, in some ways far more formal and forbidding than rituals in most churches; the oaths are sworn in the name of God on the Bible; again and again the impression is given that these are holy and awesome things. For people to take part in these things and not take them seriously is worse than believing them - it is dishonest and blasphemous. If Masons believe these things, let them say so honestly and be proud of their beliefs, not claim that they do not matter. In many ways, of course, this response reflects the increasingly irreligious culture in Britain; the language of religious faith, whether it is Christian or Masonic, is simply a foreign language to more and more people. It is hard to avoid the conclusion that the obfuscation with which Freemasonry surrounds what it does has actually contributed to that decline in religious culture.

Another response sometimes made by Masons is this: you cannot focus criticism on the rituals if you have not participated in them. In other words, the secrecy means that 'the profane' will never know what they are talking about, because the rituals are closed to them. This claim is made even though in Hannah's book and elsewhere the words of the rituals are carefully recorded and the actions described, and on the basis of this reconstructions can be acted out. While it is true that an indefinable 'atmosphere' cannot be reproduced (and this atmosphere is often claimed to be unique) it is possible to form a very clear picture from what is in print; if Masons think that the attitudes of the rest of us would change if the ceremonies were performed in public, then they could perform them in public. Perhaps they know that it would not make any difference or that we would be even more critical.

FREEMASONRY AND CATHOLIC SOCIAL TEACHING

Freemasons on the whole dispute the claim that the Craft constitutes a religion, but even if we allow this we are able to look at it in terms of what it does claim to be, 'a system of morality'. The Catholic Church teaches that *morality*, how we live our everyday lives, is at the heart of our life in Christ. The whole of part three of the *Catechism of the Catholic Church* is devoted to morality and it begins with this quotation from St Leo the Great, who was Pope in the 5th century:

'Christian, recognise your dignity and, now that you share in God's own nature, do not return to your former based condition by sinning. Remember who is your head and of whose body you are a member. Never forget that you have been rescued from the power of darkness and brought into the light of the Kingdom of God.'[43]

The Catechism goes on to say:

'Christ Jesus always did what is pleasing to the Father, and always lived in perfect communion with him. Likewise Christ's disciples are invited to live in the sight of the Father, 'who sees in secret' in order to become 'perfect as your heavenly Father is perfect'…[44]

… The way of Christ 'leads to life'; a contrary way 'leads to destruction'. The Gospel parable of the two ways remains ever present in the catechesis of the Church; it shows the importance of moral decisions for our salvation: 'There are two ways, the one of life, the other of death; but between the two, there is a great difference.'[45]

Morality and faith inseparable

For the Christian, morality is intrinsic to a life of faith. While we can discern much about moral teaching from 'natural law', by means of the use of reason, this does not mean that our moral lives can be separated from our religious beliefs or the daily life of faith. Consequently Christianity will at the outset look with suspicion at a movement which claims simply to be a 'system of morality', although as we have seen the claim that it is not a religion does not really make sense.

Christian moral teaching about our lives as individuals and about the world draws its strength from clear principles which the Church has formulated on the basis of what God has revealed and through the Christian community's reflections over many centuries. If we look at Freemasonry simply in the light of just two of these principles we can identify further problems with the movement. These two principles are important for what we call the *social teaching* of the Church - ways in which we apply moral teaching to the ordering of society.

The first is the *family*, built on marriage and centred on the procreation and upbringing of children. The Church describes the family as the 'basic cell' or 'building block' (to use a 'masonic' image) of society, reflecting not sociological accidents but the will of God the Creator:

> 'The family is the *original cell of social life*. It is the
> natural society in which husband and wife are called
> to give themselves in love and in the gift of life.'[46]

The way society is ordered, and what we do in our lives, should always nurture and strengthen families. On the face of it, Masons would probably express the strongest support for the institution and be shocked at any suggestion that their organisation undermines it.

Exclusion of women

The commitment demanded of Masons, particularly if a Mason takes it really seriously, is considerable. The setting of the Lodge very obviously takes a man away from his wife and family; except for the 'Ladies' Night' once a year, they are manifestly excluded from what happens. Short in his book describes these as 'a bribe, a guilt-ridden gift to every "Masonic widow"[47] and relays evidence from interviews with the wives of Masons which illustrates how the demands and ideology of the Craft have destroyed many marriages. Of course, there are plenty of marriages of which this is not true, and plenty of occupations amongst professional men where the stresses on family life are far more serious than in the past (and there are, of course, other organisations or professions which demand too much of people at the expense of their families), but there is something disconcerting about a demanding activity of this kind which drives a wedge between a man and those to whom he owes a particular duty of love and care, because women are categorically excluded from the most important aspects of the lodge. Short cites this old Masonic ditty which betrays a blatant misogynism:

'The ladies claim right to come into our light,
    Since the apron they say is their bearing:
Can they subject their will, can they keep their
    tongues still,
And let talking be chang'd into hearing?

This difficult task is the least we can ask,
    To secure us on sundry occasions;
When with this they comply, our utmost we'll try
    To raise lodges for lady Freemasons.

Till this can be done, must each Brother be mum,
Though the fair one should wheedle and teaze on;
Be just, true and kind; but still bear in mind,
At all times, that you are a Freemason.'[48]

No one would claim that this song has the same authority within Freemasonry as words of the rituals or charges, but it is very disturbing: the patronising attitude to women in this song contradicts so clearly what Christians believe about the equality of men and women before God, the basis for the equality, balance and mutual self-giving which should characterise marriage. We do not teach that men and women are the same, or that they should do the same things; but Masons in their ritual texts see those who are uninitiated as being incapable of attaining the light and wisdom which the Craft offers: and women are uninitiated, they are 'cowans' by their very nature.

Personal morality

If, moreover, Freemasonry is a 'system of morality', is that reflected in what is expected of the brethren in their personal lives? How does the Lodge look at adultery or infidelity in married life? From the Christian point of view marital breakdown and the sin which is usually to blame for this is one of the most serious crises in our society: we would expect an organisation like Freemasonry to take this seriously. In Short's book there

are a number of interviews with the wives or former
wives of Masons which illustrate two things: first, the
extent to which Masonic commitments made their
husbands increasingly distant from them, undermining
their marriages; and second, examples of how Masons
who were unfaithful to their wives and deserted them
encountered no censure or disciplinary action within their
lodges - nor do low standards in personal morality seem
to be a bar to admission to Freemasonry. Some might say
that we would not expect such high standards of a Golf
club, for example; but a Golf club does not claim to be a
system of morality.

Treatment of the poor

The second principle of Catholic social teaching which is
important in this study is what we call the preferential
option for the poor. This is a concept which been
important in Latin America within what is known as
Liberation Theology, but is deeply rooted in the life of the
Church and has become in recent years a clearer part of
mainstream Catholic teaching. This is how it is defined:

> 'Those who are oppressed by poverty are the object
> of a preferential love on the part of the Church
> which, since her origin and in spite of the failings of
> many of her members, has not ceased to work for
> their relief, defence and liberation…'[49]

This 'option' is about much more than charitable giving, and from this we can see how inadequate is the Masonic idea of charity which we looked at earlier. The great theologian and Patriarch of Constantinople, St John Chrysostom, put it like this:

'Not to enable the poor to share in our goods is to steal from them and deprive them of life. The goods we possess are theirs, not ours.'[50]

It is about a state of mind formed by the virtue we call *solidarity*, a state of mind which demands that we put the interests of the poor and the oppressed at the heart of our spiritual lives, and our political and social action. Pope John Paul II defined this virtue in these terms:

'This is not a feeling of vague compassion or shallow distress at the misfortunes of so many people, both near and far. On the contrary, it is *a firm and persevering determination* to commit oneself to the *common good*; that is to say to the good of all and of each individual, because we are *all* really responsible *for all*. This determination is based on the *solid* conviction that what is hindering full development is that desire for profit and that thirst for power... these attitudes and "structure of sin" are only conquered - presupposing the help of divine grace - by a *diametrically opposed attitude*: a

commitment to the good of one's neighbour with
the readiness, in the Gospel sense, to "lose oneself"
for the sake of the other instead of exploiting him,
and to "serve him" instead of oppressing him for
one's own advantage …'[51]

The Masonic view

For the Christian, solidarity is a whole way of life, a
distinctive way of thinking and of looking at the world
in which we live. It forms the whole basis not only for
the charitable work of the Catholic Church throughout
the world, but of all our social and political action. How
do we 'square' this with a religious-moral setting which
deliberately aims to restrict its membership to those
from certain classes and professions?[52] Not only that,
but the bar on discussing religion or politics in the
lodge deliberately rules out furthering understanding of
these concepts which are at the heart of morality. How
can any Christian who takes seriously the call to put the
poor at the heart of his view of society feel at home in a
setting where a poor man with his family at the lodge
door would meet the 'Tyler' with his drawn sword, not
the face of Christ? It is clear simply from looking at
Freemasonry and its social function from just two
angles in mainstream Christian moral teaching that we
simply do not believe or practice the same things. It is

of concern, of course, if other social networks which Catholics are able to join display some of the characteristics of Freemasonry.

We saw when reflecting on how Freemasonry is a 'naturalistic' religion that this means that the 'system of morality' in fact eschews the ability to be aware of absolute truths - in our path through life, it is claimed, we have 'symbols' - *and that is all*. So you are unlikely to find followers of this 'system of morality' praying outside an abortion clinic or on a CND march. Freemasonry has been particularly strong in both the medical profession and the armed forces (particularly the army), so if it has generated a culture of moral relativism in relation to the sanctity of human life we should not be surprised. The books in the 1980s written by Knight and Short are full of incidents where Masons convicted of criminal offences have not been disciplined by their lodges, let alone asked to leave: Freemasonry looks like a house, or rather a temple, built on sand.[53] Of course, the Church is full of sinners, and does not throw people out for immoral behaviour: but serious sin does have consequences, such as not being able to receive Holy Communion, and through the sacrament of Reconciliation we are offered the gift of God's forgiveness.

FREEMASONRY, HISTORY AND SOCIETY

It is often claimed that the Catholic Church's opposition to Freemasonry is political and resulting from open political warfare between the Church and Freemasonry in 19th-century Europe, particularly Italy and France. We have seen that this is not so, but we need now to look at some of the ways in which Freemasonry has operated historically in relation to the Church.

Continental Freemasonry

This booklet is about Freemasonry in Britain, and the subject of the role played by the 'Grand Orient' in much of the rest of Europe, and in Latin America, is vast and beyond our scope here; but we can make some observations. Pope Leo XIII's condemnation of Freemasonry in 1883, *Humanum Genus*, while it reiterates the theological objections which I outlined above, was clearly written in a political and historical context where the Holy See, with justification, saw Freemasonry as set on weakening the Church's influence wherever possible.[54] Those who led the armies of the Kingdom of Sardinia which took over the Papal states in 1870, and the first rulers of the Kingdom of Italy, were assertive Masons. In the long years of political battle between the Vatican and the Italian state until the signing of the Concordat with Mussolini in 1927, the Church saw Freemasonry as the heart of the problem, although ironically the freedom of the Church from temporal power has in the end increased its influence in the world in ways which Masons like Garibaldi would not have foreseen or welcomed. The ways in which the Church attacked the movement tended to portray it as a revolutionary or subversive group, partly because of its secrecy; in the whole of Italy after 1870 it quickly became the 'establishment', but in all these years there was a strong sense of its opposition to the Church. The young St Maximilian Kolbe, the Polish Franciscan later martyred at Auschwitz, was studying in Rome in 1917 during the First World War. He was profoundly affected by the public celebrations of Freemasonry's two hundredth anniversary, and he established the Knights of the Immaculate partly to counteract its influence. He wrote:

'... The Freemasons follow this principle above all: Catholicism can be overcome not by logical argument but by corrupted morals... the once-strong characters of men are weakened, families are broken up by guilt-laden hearts, and an unhealthy sorrowfulness continues to grow. When such persons are unable to shake off the miserable yoke they carry, they avoid the Church and even rise up against her.'[55]

The scandals surrounding the famous 'P2' lodge in Italy are a vast subject beyond the scope of this booklet; its subversive activities in the 1960s and 1970s are examined in Short's book.[56]

For much of this period it was even more true in France that Freemasonry was at the heart of the 'establishment'. Virtually all the cabinets of the Third Republic were dominated by Masons, and this anticlericalism brought about the rupture in relations with the Church at the beginning of the 20th century which so impoverished the clergy and excluded the Church from state provided education. In French political life the sidelining of religious beliefs to a privatised compartment is still a shared conviction among many politicians of different parties, and this can partly be attributed to the influence of Freemasonry at an earlier period.[57]

English Freemasonry

Any suggestion that Freemasonry in the British Isles is politically revolutionary can only raise a hollow laugh. From its very beginnings in the 18th century, lodges were keen to attract members of the aristocracy and the Royal Family, and they were very successful in doing so. It has been closely associated with the Royal Family - George IV, William IV, Edward VII and George VI were all Masons; the last two were very enthusiastic. The Duke of Edinburgh was initiated shortly after his marriage but has shown no interest in it; the Prince of Wales has refused to become a Freemason. The present Grand Master is the Duke of Kent, the Queen's cousin.[58] The Week of Masonic Openness in 2002 seems to have been linked to the celebrations of the Queen's Golden Jubilee, and Masonic events often conclude with the singing of the national anthem.

This link with the monarchy illustrates how English-speaking Freemasonry has always been associated with the most powerful in society (this is equally true in the United States, where Franklin and Washington were both Masons, as have been many Presidents). Knight's and Short's books have examined in great detail the extent of Masonic influence in the Law, the Public schools, Medicine, public utilities, architecture and building, Parliament, all levels of local government, the security services, the City of London, the Army and, above all, the Police. If only a fraction of the allegations made in these sources is true, we see in Freemasonry a network of men keen on being amongst the most powerful and wealthy elements in the life of this country, bound by a primary loyalty to each other. The scandals brought to light in the 1980s, particularly those in the Metropolitan police and in Derbyshire[59] ought to alarm Catholics and others who care about standards of integrity in public life, even decades later. The obsession with money and privilege which is evident from what has been written and the concentration of the Craft in the middle and upper classes speak of a view of the world at odds with Christian teaching about human dignity and the poor. Lodges claim not to be political, but there is an overwhelming identification visible between the Craft and political conservatism: it is still in the Court pages of The Daily Telegraph that Masonic activities are reported. This identification of the Craft with the established order is enshrined in one of its official documents, *The Universal Book of Craft Masonry*:

> 'Freemasonry…distinctly enjoins us to respect all social distinctions, so that while some must rule, others must obey and cheerfully accept their inferior positions.'[60]

This is a long way from Our Lady's *Magnificat*, which the Church prays every day at Evening Prayer:

> 'He has routed the proud of heart. He has pulled down princes from their thrones and exalted the lowly. The hungry he has filled with good things, the rich sent empty away.'[61]

We saw earlier that one of the characteristics of Freemasonry, made explicit in its obligations and charges, is the Mason's obligation to come to the help of his brother Mason. In theory this is not meant to be absolute, and infringing civil laws is ruled out, but the scandals which have come to light show that frequently this group loyalty has acted in a corrupt way.

Discrimination

All the allegations made over the years, which have not been refuted, of special favours and corruption should concern Catholics because of what we believe about society, but there is another reason why this is a problem: the corruption has often led to discrimination against those who are not Masons and against Catholics in particular. In the troubled history of Northern Ireland, the most important grievance against the Royal Ulster Constabulary was that the organisation discriminated against Catholics: clear evidence in Short's book shows that this was linked to the strength within the RUC and among middle-class Protestants of Freemasonry. The police forces in Lancashire, Merseyside and Greater Manchester up to the 1980s showed similar signs of anti-Catholicism linked to the Craft.[62] Most Catholic parishes will have people who can testify to discrimination against them as a result of Masonic influence. Indeed, one reason for the setting up of the *Catenian Association* was to provide a network of support for Catholic men in professional and business life to counteract discrimination at the hands of Freemasons[63] and the picture is far too widespread for it to be inaccurate paranoia. Moreover the strength of the Craft in local government, particularly in authorities controlled by the Conservative party[64], has often led to political decisions at odds with the interests of the Church. For example, in one outer London borough there is a strong feeling among Catholics that over the years the building of new Catholic schools and the provision of facilities for existing ones has at times been impaired by anti-Catholic feeling resulting from the local strength of Freemasonry; similarly there have been instances of Catholic institutions and individuals losing money as a result of hostile planning decisions.[65]

However, as Catholics we should be careful about giving too much emphasis to discrimination that our community has suffered as a result of the hostility of Masons - Jesus told his disciples that this would happen, and he exhorted us to 'rejoice and dance for joy' because of it.[66] We should also be aware that it is clear that things have improved. First of all, Freemasonry is in trouble and in decline. Figures have never been easy to work out[67] but it seems that active membership is now down to 320,000[68]; initiatives like the Week of Openness and a much more outgoing public relations approach suggest not only a wish to respond to the scandals and the criticism but a need to recruit younger members. The decline in membership is not unique to the Masons, but reflects a widespread decline in the membership of clubs, societies, churches and political parties. Another reason must be that men have less to gain than in the past from being Masons because of the scandals. As a result of what came to light twenty years ago, there is more pressure on figures in public life now to have to reveal Masonic membership, so the networks of control in local government and the police, which Knight and Short identified, are weaker.[69]

Anti-Christian

When we look at the role played by Freemasonry in society, we will draw the conclusion that, in spite of the good moral qualities of many of its members, it has often had a baleful and anti-Christian influence. It is clear that this is not only because of evidence of opposition to the Church and discrimination against Catholics, but even more because it does not speak of God's love for the poor, but rather of the 'self-made' man who has done well in the world and who believes that he should be rewarded as much as possible. There is a revealing quotation from a Mason in Short's book which casts light on the well known prohibition against discussing religion or politics in the lodge: 'There's be no point in talking about religion because most Masons know nothing about it. As for politics, they don't need to talk about it. They're nearly all Conservatives.'[70]

FREEMASONRY AND OTHER CHRISTIAN CHURCHES

This booklet is intended primarily for Roman Catholics
and looks at Freemasonry in the light of Roman Catholic
teaching. But for the most part the reasons why Catholics
cannot be Masons are the same as those which have
prompted every Christian church which has ever looked
into the Craft to form a critical view. Catholics are
committed to the belief that it is the work of the Holy
Spirit that Christians are much closer and less divided
than in the past, and the growth in ecumenism has
coincided with a growing consensus about the
relationship between Christianity and Freemasonry; so it
is helpful to look at the position of other churches,
especially as the fundamental reasons are not peculiar to
Catholic Christianity.

Church of England Report

The consensus has not always been present. Until the
1980s the leadership of the Church of England had
largely failed, as a result of the influence of Masons
among its senior clergy, to conduct any examination of
whether faithful Anglicans could be Masons. When
Hannah wrote his book in the 1950s a very large number

of bishops all over the Anglican Communion were Masons, including Dr Geoffrey Fisher, the Archbishop of Canterbury, and he records his unsuccessful efforts to engage in dialogue with them about the issue (Hannah subsequently became a Catholic). The Church of England, following the publication of Knight's book, did debate the issue in the mid 1980s and it is significant that by that time the most senior Mason among the Anglican hierarchy who could be found to defend the Craft was a cathedral dean rather than a bishop. The General Synod of the Church of England set up a working party to look at the issue, which in 1987 produced the report *Christianity and Freemasonry - are they compatible?*[71]

The majority of those on the working party (there were two Masons on the working party who dissented from many of the criticisms) were critical of Freemasonry, particularly of the Royal Arch, and felt that there is a clear Pelagian 'salvation by works' theology in the rituals. These are the concluding sentences of the report:

'The reflections of the Working Group itself reveal understandable differences of opinion between those who are Freemasons and those who are not. Whilst the former fully agree that the Report shows that there are clear difficulties to be faced by Christians who are Freemasons, the latter are of the mind that the Report points to a number of very fundamental reasons to question the compatibility of Freemasonry with Christianity'[72]

But the synod (after a response from Grand Lodge) in its subsequent debate failed to give definite guidance as to what Anglicans should do - it was merely accepted and commended for further discussion.[73] When Dr Rowan Williams was appointed Archbishop of Canterbury in 2003 his own concerns about it became public[74], and it is obvious that the Craft is much weaker in the Church of England than at any time in its history. There are many reasons for this: it is weaker in society in general, the Church of England is less influential in society than in the past, and within the Church of England the Evangelical movement is much stronger than in the past: in churches of all traditions there is far more emphasis than in the past on personal faith and commitment, since going to church is nowadays a matter of choice rather than social convention. Moreover, all the churches are more committed both to ecumenism involving Catholics and to social justice: the Church of England is far less identified with those with real power or influence in our society than in the past. Those with the attitudes we have identified within the Craft are likely to feel less at home in a church than in the past.

Cathedrals

There are still some signs of strength, especially in relation to cathedrals. In 2002, as part of celebrations to do with the 'Week of Masonic Openness', a special act of worship was held in St Paul's cathedral, at which the Dean preached. Masonic lodges and provinces have always given generously to cathedrals, no doubt because of the work of 'operative' Masons in building them.[75] At least as far as medieval foundations are concerned it is surely legitimate for Catholics to express concern about these gifts. Anglican cathedrals attempt to carry out an important ministry for the whole community, not simply Anglicans who attend their services; moreover, medieval cathedrals are surely part of the shared inheritance of all Christians in this country, which is partly the reason why permission has been given for occasional celebrations of the Catholic Mass in them in recent years. Consequently Catholics and members of the Free churches are entitled to ask questions with sensitivity about Masonic gifts to cathedrals or Masonic acts of worship. (It should be borne in mind that on the whole Grand Lodge, because of criticisms in the past, does not permit now distinctively Masonic acts of worship or Masonic funerals in churches). In addition to the relationship with cathedrals there are signs that in areas where Freemasonry is still strong its members are still to be found in some Anglican churches, and they can be particularly influential in small congregations. What is rather surprising is that Masons are sometimes to be found in churches with an Anglo-Catholic tradition, which share many beliefs and liturgical traditions with the Catholic Church, and where there is strong desire for reunion with the Holy See.

The Free Churches

The Free churches have on the whole been critical of Freemasonry for much longer. Before the Anglican enquiry the Methodist Conference adopted a report which stated clearly, 'Methodists should not become Freemasons' and banned lodges from meeting on Methodist premises. The report also said 'There is a great danger that the Christian who becomes a Freemason will find himself compromising his Christian beliefs or his allegiance to Christ, perhaps without realising what he is doing'[75]. Hannah in his book in the 1950s pointed out how many Free churches, including the Salvation Army, had condemned Freemasonry, and the same has been true for many years of the Eastern Orthodox churches. An official statement from the Church of Scotland in 1965 stated 'In our view total obedience to Christ precludes joining an organisation such as the Masonic movement which seems to demand a wholehearted allegiance to itself, and at the same time refuses to divulge all that is involved in that allegiance prior to joining.'[76]

As he says, 'One startling fact emerges, which should make the Christian Mason more than a little thoughtful. *No Church that has seriously investigated the religious teachings and implications of Freemasonry has ever yet failed to condemn it.*'[78]

It is important in the search for greater unity among Christians that we are all able to be open with each other: so if we raise concerns about Freemasonry in other churches it would be contrary to the spirit of ecumenism for people to say to us, 'It's none of your business,' especially if the remaining presence of Freemasonry in different churches is an impairment to closer relations between churches. A spirit of openness is not easy to find with regard to an organisation like Freemasonry, although it is more open than in the past; but in local 'Churches Together' groups, Catholics should certainly raise the issue with sensitivity in discussions if it is thought that Freemasonry is strong in other churches, particularly if there is a history of anti-Catholic prejudice in an area which can be attributed to the Craft's influence. There is also likely to be concern if *clergy* of other churches are Freemasons. In all this, Christians from different traditions can learn a great deal from each other and share good practice.

There is, however, a more disturbing question. Why should any Christian, in view of what we have examined about the Craft, *want* to be a Mason? What does it say about the nature of faith within our communities? Perhaps in all the churches we can still see ways in which we have failed to instil in one another a strong enough personal faith, and a sense in which a church operates as a loving and supportive community.

What to do if you are a Catholic
and a Freemason

It is likely that in the late 1970s a number of Catholics in
Britain and the United States became Masons in good
faith and with what seemed to be Episcopal approval, and
also possible that some have been unaware of the
reiteration of the traditional position in 1983. If this
applies to anyone reading this booklet, the position is
clear: if you are a Mason and aware of the Church's
teaching you are in a state of objectively grave sin and
may not receive Holy Communion. The only way you can
remedy this is to resign from your lodge and then go to
confession. Some of you reading this may have Catholic
relatives to whom this may apply, so it is important that
you pass this booklet on to them, raising the issue calmly
and gently.

   If you are a Mason and exploring becoming a Catholic,
you will need to relinquish your Masonic membership
before you are baptised or received into the Church. In
both these instances it is not enough simply to be an
'inactive' Mason: you have to resign. Do not be alarmed
by those who tell you that your Masonic oaths will still
be binding if you resign: they are not, as far as Christian

moral teaching is concerned, for the reasons outlined above. Moreover it makes no difference that in different periods of history Catholics have been Masons, such as Mozart, Haydn or Daniel O'Connell (in the early part of his career[79]): the position of the Church in our own time is crystal clear.

There is evidence of how men who have been embroiled in Freemasonry have sometimes experienced psychological problems, their minds filled with violence and fear.[80] The rituals will often cause a variety of reactions, and it may be that reading this booklet has made you more aware of the problem. If this is so you should talk to a priest and pray with him for deliverance from what may be troubling you.

Summarising the Key Considerations

Some Christian critics of Freemasonry have found it helpful to see the 'system' as three concentric circles. The outer circle, which is the largest, is composed of men who are really only interested in its charitable and social activities; the middle circle is made up of those in Freemasonry who have power and influence because they have money; those in the middle are those who are most committed to its ideology, rituals and world-view.[81] The reasons why the churches are entitled to be concerned about Christians who are Masons is that even if they are only in the outer circle they are still part of the whole system and organisation.

The Catholic Church believes that we should show tolerance and respect towards members of other faiths, asserted in the Second Vatican Council's Declaration on Religious Freedom, *Dignitatis Humanae* (1965). It may well be the case that in previous periods of history, when Christians were lacking this mutual tolerance, Freemasonry enabled people from different backgrounds to relate to each other; but the trouble is that this was done by teaching that the differences were of no consequence. But the teaching as presented by the Council does mean that we should affirm the freedom of Masons to worship according to their consciences, just as we should in relation to Jews, Muslims, Hindus and others. But this demands that we see it for what it really is, a religion in its right. It will not be easy for us - or anyone else - to put any respect into practice for as long as Freemasonry denies its essential character as a religion, or for as long as so many Masons say that the rituals are meaningless and that they only go along for the social life or the charitable giving; and you cannot have 'dual membership' of incompatible religions. Moreover, since Freemasonry has effectively and deliberately undermined essential truths of Christian teaching among its members who have been Christians, our respect for the institution as a whole, as opposed to individual members, will be limited compared to the view we have of other world religions.

There are signs that Grand Lodge is aware that the obsessive secrecy is part of the problem they face, and as already mentioned, in 2003 hired a public relations expert who is not a Mason to improve their image.[82] You can even buy some of the classic attacks on Freemasonry from the shops opposite Freemasons' Hall in Covent Garden. But the 'openness' has its limits: while you can find out the names of Grand and Provincial officers very easily, you cannot find out who the members or officials are of individual lodges.

Above all, we should be aware of two things:

1) The heart of what we believe about salvation and enlightenment is exclusive faith in Jesus Christ, the Word made flesh. It is the work of God's Holy Spirit that fewer and fewer Christians in this country attempt to be Masons as well, because this is the result of deeper reflection on the unique claims we make in relation to Christ.

2) What sets Christians at odds with the Craft is in itself a symbol of what sets us at odds with much of British society: that the God we worship is the God of the poor and oppressed: God loves and cares about those who are rich, but exhorts them to humble themselves, detach themselves from their wealth and share their wealth with the poor: Christianity does not identify with many of the

values in our culture of the successful, 'self made' man with standing in society who has money and privilege.

Urging Masons to deal with us all 'on the level', and helping Christians to understand the differences between our faith and Freemasonry, should enable all of us to be more aware of the truths at the heart of our beliefs as Christians within the family of the Catholic Church.

ENDNOTES

1 Chulmleigh: Augustine publishing co., 3rd ed.,1963, referred to in these notes as 'Hannah'.

2 London: Collins, 1985, referred to as 'Knight'.

3 London: Collins, 1989, referred to as 'Short'. A second edition was published in 1995.

4 From the ceremony of raising to the 'second degree', Hannah p. 115.

5 Used in a town council meeting in Bournemouth in 1981, described by Short p.429.

6 Ceremony of raising to the third degree, Hannah p.141.

7 The details are given in Short pp.18ff.

8 Stephen Moss, 'Secrets and Ties', *The Guardian*, 21 March 2001. Another example would the publication of a defence of Freemasonry by a non-Mason, Jasper Ridley, in The Freemasons (London: Robinson, 2000).

9 An example of how this was promoted was a leaflet, 'Getting to Know You', published by the Province of West Kent, detailing family activities and charitable work. This leaflet was made available in at least one public library in the London Borough of Bromley.

10 *Acta Apostolicae Sedis* 73 (1981), 220-224.

11 *Acta Apostolicae Sedis* 76 (1984), 300, author's translation.

12 In Denzinger-Schonmetzer, *Enchiridion Symbolorum Definitionum et Declarationum de rebus fidei et morum* (36th ed., Barcelona: Herder, 1976; 'DS'), 2511-2513. This is a translation of parts of the letter: 'We have been aware for a long time and in many places that there are coming into being and growing stronger day by day some societies, assemblies, clubs and groupings or gatherings which are popularly known as *Free builders* or *Free Masons* - or called by other similar names in various languages. In these groups men from various religions or sects... are bound together in tightly knit and impassable

leagues. They are regulated by laws and rules which they have set up for themselves - laws which are secret and are made binding by means of oaths on the sacred Bible, and are kept hidden by the imposition of grave penalties... We should watch out lest men of this kind dig through the human race like thieves, perverting the hearts of simple people...'

[13] Those which followed were Benedict XIV, *Providus* (1751) Pius VII, *Ecclesiam*, (1821), Leo XII, *Quo Graviora* (1825) and Blessed Pius IX, *Qui Pluribus* (1846), *Quibus Quantisque* (1849), *Nostis et Nobiscum* (1849) *Quanta Cura* (1864), *Multiplices Inter* (1865), *Apostolicae Sedis* (1869) and *Etsi Multa Luctuosa* (1873; no.1841 in earlier editions of Denzinger but omitted in the 1976 edition). We will look at Leo XIII's *Humanum Genus* below. The Holy See also issued specific instructions to Catholics in various countries forbidding them from becoming Masons, including one for England and Ireland dated 2 July 1845.

[14] Canon 2335.

[15] *Code of Canon Law* (1983), 1374. For details of the drafting history see *The Canon Law - Letter and Spirit* (London: Geoffrey Chapman 1995), pp.791 - 792.

[16] Dated 19 July 1974. The details can be found in the report by Professor William Whalen for the Committee for Pastoral research and Practices of the Catholic Bishops Conference of the United States, published in Charles Madden, OFM Conv., *Freemasonry - Mankind's Hidden Enemy* (Rockford: Tan books, 1995), p.37.

[17] quoted in Knight p.250.

[18] Short records that as part of the celebrations that the rift had been healed in NewYork Cardinal Terence Cooke in 1976 addressed a 'Masonic Dedication Breakfast' and spoke of the 'road of friendship between the Masons and the Catholics of America.' (p.156).

[19] 'Irreconcilability between Christian faith and Freemasonry', 11 March 1985.

[20] Appendices C and D in Madden, op.cit., pp. 33ff. The position in England and Wales was also made clear in the 'Dear Anne' column in *The Universe*, 23 March 1984, p.32.

21 Current Direction on Membership, *Masonic Year Book* 2000-1.

22 Hannah p.124.

23 Hannah p.132.

24 Hannah p.137.

25 DS 3156-3158; this extract is quoted in Madden, op.cit. p. 45.

26 This is a very well known hymn, written by W. Chambers Smith (1824-1908). In 1988 Grand Lodge produced a promotional video about Freemasonry in which thousands of brethren are depicted singing this hymn in the Albert Hall. It contains no reference to Christ.

27 *Amtsblatt des Erbistums Koln*, June 1980, quoted in Madden, op.cit., p.48.

28 On all this see Short chapter 37,'Charity Begins at Home', pp. 607ff. He points out that many of the non-Masonic causes are actually linked to Freemasonry or to leading Freemasons.

29 Hannah p.53, For example see
    http://surreymason.org.uk/charity_prov_festival_jewel.htm.

30 Matthew 6:1-4 (Jerusalem Bible).

31 Hannah p.135.

32 Hannah p.217.

33 Hannah p.95.

34 Knight p.27. On the de-Christianisation see Knight chapter 3, 'Schism and Reunion', pp.25ff., and Short chapter 2, 'Whatever Happened to Jesus?', pp.66ff.

35 Short p.145 points out that the one exception may be the phrase 'bright morning star' which still appears in the rituals, such as the charge in the raising to the third degree. On the face of it this refers to Christ and seems to be taken from Revelation 22:16, 'I am of David's line, the root of David and the bright star of the morning.' It seems odd that this reference was not removed when other Christian references were taken out. As Short shows it is possible that it does not refer to Our Lord at all, but to 'Lucifer', the fallen angel, for whom this title is also used. Lucifer is commonly identified with Satan, and this interpretation makes Masonic worship even more

disturbing from a Christian point of view. It is recorded that in demonstrations against the Church at the beginning of the 20th century by Masons in Italy banners were carried depicting the Archangel Michael being trodden underfoot by Lucifer (Madden,op.cit., p.30) and in Italian Freemasonry a *Hymn to Satan* seems to have been popular (P. J. Chandlery SJ, *Pilgrim Walks in Rome* [Roehampton: Manresa Press 1924], p. 348).

36 Short p.105. It is difficult to imagine what the ritual must be like without one of its most important elements. Short describes the long debate with Grand Chapter (the supreme body of Royal Arch Freemasonry) about this following the publication of the Church of England report which singled out this question: even the two Masons on the working party were unhappy with this aspect of Royal Arch ritual. Appendix IX of the Anglican General Synod report (note 71 below; pp. 52-55) gives details of the alternative to the traditional 'names' in the ritual proposed by Canon Richard Tydeman.

37 Hannah p.206. The Rose Croix is really seen as an 'elite among elites' in Freemasonry.

38 Short pp.147-8.

39 Madden, op.cit. p.8 points out that in the 30th degree of the 'Scottish Rite', the 'Grand Elected Knights Kadosh' the initiation rite involves the stabbing and trampling of a mock papal tiara. These degrees are popular in American Freemasonry.

40 Roman Missal, Preface of Sundays in Ordinary Time I.

41 Canons 1199 and 1200. See also the commentary on this in *Canon Law - Letter and Spirit* p. 681.

42 Hannah p.24 quotes on this the view in the 1950s of Canon V. A. Demant, Regius Professor of Moral and Pastoral Theology at Oxford University: 'Looking at the nature of the vows in general, it does seem very difficult for a Churchman to undertake them without being guilty of either vain (*vanum*) or rash (*temerarium*) swearing. He seems to be initiated into an alien cult. If it is not taken seriously - or taken very symbolically (in contravention of the oath's words:

without evasion, equivocation, or mental reservation of any kind)
then the oath comes under the heading of vain swearing or profanity.
If it is taken seriously then it must be put down as rash swearing, for
there is no certainty that the Christian initiate will not find afterwards
that he has joined an alien cult.'

43 *Catechism of the Catholic Church* (rev.ed., London: Geoffrey
Chapman 1999) 1691, quoting *Sermo 21 in Nat. Domini* 3, PL
54.192C.

44 1693.

45 1696.

46 Catechism 2207.

47 P. 641.

48 Pp. 641-2. This recalls these lines spoken by the priests in *The Magic
Flute*: 'Beware of womanly wiles; this is the brotherhood's first duty.
Many a wise man has been beguiled, has erred and not realised it..'
(Act 2, scene 3) and 'The sacred portals are desecrated! Down to hell
with these women!'(scene 5) It perhaps of some significance that when
a man is initiated into Freemasonry he has to remove all metal objects
on his person, including his wedding ring if he has one. Of course,
other organisations, including some within the Catholic Church, do not
admit women; perhaps in some cases this will change as cultural
attitudes change, but what we can discern in Freemasonry is an
ideology with regard to this exclusion which is altogether different.

49 Sacred Congregation for the Doctrine of the Faith, Instruction
Libertatis Conscientia (1986),68, quoted in Catechism 2448. Like the
instruction on Freemasonry this was published under the name of the
congregation's Prefect, Cardinal Joseph Ratzinger, now Pope
Benedict XVI.

50 *Hom. in Lazarum* 2.5, PG 48.992, quoted in Catechism 2446.

51 Encyclical letter *Sollicitudo Rei Socialis* (1987), 38.

52 Masonic lodges in the United States are racially segregated. Black
men cannot join 'mainstream' lodges and their own parallel system of
'Prince Hall' lodges is not recognised by 'regular' Freemasonry. The

same was true in *apartheid* South Africa. These mainstream lodges have close links with Grand Lodge in England. In the 19th century Freemasons in the United States were also responsible for founding the openly racist and criminal Ku Klux Klan and gave the Klan many of its rituals. On all this see William J. Whalen, *Christianity and American Freemasonry* (Bruce, Milwaukee: 1958; Huntingdon, Indiana: Our Sunday Visitor, Inc., 1987).

[53] For instances of marital breakdown, sometimes as a result of infidelity, see Short chapter 39. For Freemasonry's strength in the medical profession and in the forces, especially the army, see Short chapter 29, 'What's Up, Doc?' and chapter 31, 'The Regimental Square'.

[54] A similar historical context involving English Masons in Florence seems to have existed when the first condemnation was issued by Pope Clement XII, *In Eminenti*, in 1738 (note 12 above). But it is not correct to claim that this means that the basis of the condemnation, and subsequent papal statements, were political rather than theological.

[55] Madden, op.cit., p.30.

[56] Chapter 33, 'Spooks in Aprons', pp.532ff.

[57] Short p.154. and pp.164-5 shows similar efforts at a *rapprochement* between the Catholic Church and Freemasonry in France. It is interesting to note in passing the controversy about the omission of any reference to God or the Christian faith in the draft Constitutional Treaty of the European Union agreed in 2004, about which the Catholic Church made strong representations: the convenor of the convention which drafted it, former French President Valery Giscard D'Estaing, is a Mason.

[58] Knight chapter 23, 'The Highest in the Land', pp.211ff. The Queen has an honorific role of patronage and protection. It seems that both the Queen Mother and Lord Mountbatten were strongly opposed to Freemasonry.

[59] Short chapter 12, 'The Fall and Fall of Brian Woollard' and chapter 20, 'Parrish's Council.'

[60] Knight p.309.

[61]   Luke 1:51-53.

[62]   Short chapter 19, 'The Encompassing of John Stalker', especially pp.330ff. I have been given a more recent example. Claims are still made that in criminal incidents which can be linked to Masons officers in local police forces behave unethically.

[63]   In spite of this history, there has been correspondence in recent years in the letters column of the association magazine *Catena* about whether Catholics can become Masons; it is also claimed that in some places joint social events have taken place. The *Catenian Association* is sometimes lightheartedly and unfairly seen by some as a 'Catholic Freemasonry'. When Freemasons in public life have been pressurised to make their membership of the organisation known, they have sometimes demanded the same of members of the Catenians, the Knights of St Columba, and Opus Dei.

[64]   This is outlined by Short in chapters 26, 'Masonic Light in Town Halls', 27, 'London Belongs to Them' and 34, 'The Tory Party in Aprons'. Prior to the growth in strength of the 'Left' in the Labour party in local government since the 1970s, many Labour councillors were Masons as well, but that has not been true since then and Labour authorities have led calls for Masonic membership to be made publicly known.

[65]   This is anecdotal evidence relayed to me, going back many years, with regard to the London Borough of Bromley. It should be stressed that this does not relate to recent years and that there is very little sign of anti-Catholic bias now within the authority.

[66]   Luke 6:21.

[67]   Short chapter 9, 'Figuring the Facts', pp. 170ff.

[68]   *The Guardian*, art.cit.

[69]   In 1994 and 1995 the Home Affairs Select Committee of the House of Commons, chaired by Chris Mullin MP, held a number of hearings as part of an enquiry into the role of Freemasonry in the police and the judiciary. Among those who testified to the committee were Martin Short and the then Grand Secretary of the United Grand

Lodge of England, Commander Michael Higham. The committee in its report recommended that police officers and judges be required to reveal Masonic membership. As legislation has not followed this has only happened on a voluntary basis since, unevenly. There is a requirement in the National Assembly for Wales for members to register membership of the Freemasons in the assembly's statutory register of interests. In the current register no assembly members are listed as being Masons.

70 Short pp. 185-186.

71 Church House publishing: London 1987.

72 Quoted in Short pp.86-87.

73 Short p. 88.

74 Jason Bennetto, 'New Archbishop: Masons have no place in the Church', *The Independent*, 15 November 2002. The subsequent correspondence between Grand Lodge and Dr Williams can be read on http://www.cesnur.org/2003/coe.htm; the archbishop makes it clear that while his views were misrepresented, he does have concerns in particular about clergy being Masons. At the time of writing a report is expected later in 2005 by Caroline Windsor, *Freemasonry and the Ministry*, which will examine the effects Freemasonry has on the ordained ministry of the Church of England (as reported in 'Facing up to Freemasonry' *Church of England Newspaper*, 9 September 2005). Among critiques of Freemasonry from those within the Evangelical tradition in the Church of England see J. Lawrence, *Freemasonry - a religion?* (London: Kingsway 1987). Another recent examination is G. Mather and L. A. Nichols, *Masonic Lodge* (*Zondervan Guide to Cults and Religious Movements*, 1st series, Carlisle 1995).

75 There are details given in Short, pp.613ff. In 2002 the West Kent Province helped to pay for a mural depicting the Baptism of Christ for Rochester Cathedral. The leaflet referred to in note 9 above gives the impression that the Masons had been solely responsible for paying for the mural.

76 Short pp.81ff has the first quotation; the second is cited in *Church of*

England Newspaper, art.cit. Freemasonry is still strong within Methodism in Nigeria. I am grateful to Fr Victor Akongwale for this information.

[77] Hannah pp. 70ff. The Church of Scotland report is quoted in *Church of England Newspaper,* art.cit.

[78] Hannah p.78.

[79] Short pp.231-232.

[80] Short pp.144ff.

[81] I am grateful to Fr Michael Gwinnell for this point.

[82] *The Guardian,* art.cit.

Compendium of the

CATECHISM OF THE
CATHOLIC CHURCH

"*The Compendium*, which I now present to the Universal Church, is a faithful and sure synthesis of the

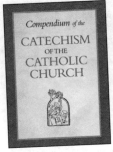

Catechism of the Catholic Church. It contains, in concise form, all the essential and fundamental elements of the Church's faith, thus constituting, as my Predecessor had wished, a kind of *vademecum*, which allows believers and non-believers alike to behold the entire panorama of the Catholic faith."

Benedictus PP XVI

ISBN: 978 1 86082 376 3

CTS Code: Do 742

Understanding the New Age Movement

The New Age Movement is regarded by many Christians as a growing threat to traditional beliefs and practices. Why are so many people attracted to astrology, reincarnation and magic, to spiritualism and goddess-worship, to new cults and old heresies? This clear and thoroughly researched text explores the meaning and direction of the New Age Movement in relation to Catholic teaching, and asks how Catholics can best respond to the challenge it represents.

Stratford Caldecott is the author of *Catholic Social Teaching: A Way In*.

ISBN: 978 1 86082 408 1

CTS Code: Ex 23

Jehovah's Witnesses

An incisive analysis of the beliefs of Jehovah's Witnesses and of the Watchtower Society. John Wijngaards, with courtesy and compassion, explains the falsity of their interpretation of Scripture, their beliefs and practices, and in particular of the untrustworthy and misguided teachings of their leaders. He encourages Jehovah's Witnesses to listen to reasoned argument and face the truth. An excellent booklet for all concerned about or having contact with Jehovah's Witnesses.

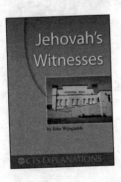

ISBN: 978 1 86082 040 3

CTS Code: Ex 02